# Vietnam

## Denise Allard

A ZOË BOOK

## A *ZOË BOOK*

© 1996 Zoë Books Limited

Devised and produced by
Zoë Books Limited
15 Worthy Lane
Winchester
Hampshire SO23 7AB
England

First published in Great Britain in 1996 by
Zoë Books Limited
15 Worthy Lane
Winchester
Hampshire SO23 7AB

A record of the CIP data is available from the British Library.

ISBN 1 874488 84 3

Printed in Italy by Grafedit SpA
Editor: Kath Davies
Design: Sterling Associates
Map: Julian Baker
Production: Grahame Griffiths

**Photographic acknowledgments**

The publishers wish to acknowledge, with thanks, the following photographic sources:

FLPA / Terry Whittaker 22; Explorer / Robert Harding Picture Library - cover bl; The Hutchison Library / Robert Francis 6; / Felix Greene 14; / Sarah Murray 28; Impact Photos / Mark Henley - cover tl & r, 12, 18, 26; / Christopher Pillitz - title page; / Material World 8; / Caroline Penn 10, 20; / Andy Solomon 16; Frank Spooner Pictures 24.

# Contents

All the words that appear in **bold** are explained in the Glossary on page 30.

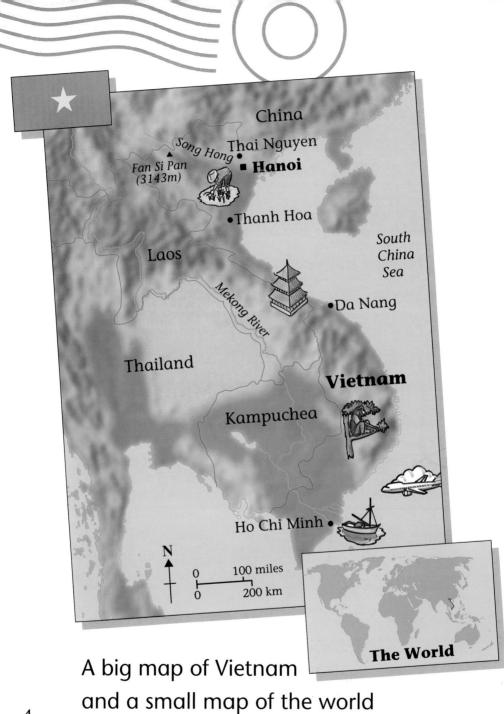

China

Thai Nguyen

Song Hong

Fan Si Pan
(3143m)

■ **Hanoi**

•Thanh Hoa

Laos

South
China
Sea

Mekong River

•Da Nang

Thailand

**Vietnam**

Kampuchea

Ho Chi Minh •

N

| 0 | 100 miles |
| 0 | 200 km |

**The World**

A big map of Vietnam
and a small map of the world

Dear Sally,

You can see Vietnam in red on the small map. It is a long way from home. The plane took more than 11 hours to fly here from London. The weather in Vietnam is hot and wet.

Love,

Pat

**P.S.** Dad says that more than half of Vietnam is made up of mountains and forests. About 74 million people live in Vietnam. Most people live on the flat lands beside the coast.

Beside a lake near the middle of Hanoi

Dear Mel,

We are staying in Hanoi. It is the **capital** city of Vietnam. We can see this big lake from our hotel. There is a special building called a **pagoda** near the lake.

Love,

Dan

**P.S.** Today we saw the burial place of a man called Ho Chi Minh. He is buried in Hanoi. Mum says that Ho Chi Minh was a famous leader of the Vietnamese people.

A family meal at home in the city of Thai Nguyen

Dear Chancie,

The food here is very tasty. We have fresh vegetables and rice with every meal. People in Vietnam do not use knives and forks. They eat their food with **chopsticks**.

Your friend,

Ali

P.S.  People in Vietnam buy food at the markets. They buy fruit and vegetables which are grown on farms. People pay for the food with Vietnamese money called *dong*.

The Hoi An Temple near Da Nang

Dear Luke,

We have seen lots of **temples** in Vietnam. A temple is a holy place. People who follow the **Buddhist** religion visit the temples to pray. Most of the temples are very old.

Love,

Sonia

**P.S.** Most people here speak only Vietnamese. It sounds a little like Chinese. Dad says that more than 1,000 years ago, China ruled Vietnam.

A family in a tri-shaw, Hanoi

Dear Samantha,

Many people in Vietnam ride bicycles. They use bicycles to travel everywhere. We went for a ride in a **tricycle** taxi, called a tri-shaw. It took us around the city of Hanoi.

Love,

Gemma

**P.S.** Mum says that people in Vietnam travel around the country by train. There are river boats to carry goods between the cities.

Farmers at work in the rice fields

Dear Rob,

We are in the countryside near Thanh Hoa. Many people work hard in the fields. The rice plants grow best in a lot of water. The farmers get very wet while they work.

Love,

Fran

**P.S.** Dad says that rice is a very useful **crop**. People here eat a lot of rice. They use the dried rice stalks to make paper, sandals, hats and baskets.

Landing a catch of fish

Dear Bruno,

These fishermen catch a lot of fish. They also catch lobsters and shrimps from the South China Sea. Most fishing boats go out at night. They come back in the morning.

See you soon,

Brad

**P.S.** Mum says that people in Vietnam like to eat fish. They eat fish from the sea and fish from the rivers. Some of the fish is sold to other countries.

A busy market near the railway station in the city of Ho Chi Minh

Dear Laura,

We are in the city called Ho Chi Minh. There are lots of shops and street stalls here. You can buy all kinds of things. We bought some baskets and pots to take home with us.

Your friend,

Alex

**P.S.** Dad says that about 40 years ago, Vietnam was divided into two parts. At that time Ho Chi Minh city was called Saigon. Saigon was the capital city of South Vietnam.

Embroidering a tablecloth

Dear Jane,

Mum bought some tablecloths from this shop. They were all **embroidered** by hand. She bought some shiny, red pots too. They are made with a kind of glue called lacquer.

Love,

Seb

**P.S.** Mum says that the lacquer in Vietnam comes from the Son Tree. The artist uses the lacquer to make a pattern on the pot. Some of the patterns are very beautiful.

Langur monkeys from the forests
of Vietnam

Dear Imran,

The mountains in Vietnam are covered in forests. All kinds of animals and birds live in the forests. Now people are cutting down the trees. The animals and birds may lose their homes.

Your friend,

Guy

**P.S.** Dad says that **native** peoples live in the forests too. They move around from place to place. They live far away from other people.

Judo practice at a special sports school

Dear Ray,

I have a friend in Vietnam. He does a lot of **judo**. He goes to a special school for children who are good at sports. At school he also plays table tennis. He does **gymnastics** too.

Your friend,

Lisa

**P.S.** Mum says that people in Vietnam like **traditional** sports such as swordfighting with wooden sticks. They also enjoy gentle exercises called 'Tai chi'.

Dragon dancers in Ho Chi Minh city

Dear Kirsty,

I hope you like these dragon dancers. All over Vietnam, people dress up and dance to welcome the New Year. Every town and village enjoys this special **festival**.

Love,

Craig

**P.S.** Dad says that there are many festivals in Vietnam. Some of them are part of the people's religion. Other festivals are for people who like music or the theatre.

The flag of Vietnam flying over
Ho Chi Minh's burial place in Hanoi

Dear Mari,

The flag of Vietnam is red. It has a gold star in the middle. The people of North Vietnam have used this flag since 1945. At that time Ho Chi Minh was the leader of North Vietnam.

Love,

Judy

**P.S.** Mum says that Vietnam is a **republic**. This means that the people of Vietnam choose their own rulers. The head of the country is called the president.

# Glossary

**Buddhists**: People who follow the teachings of the Buddha. He lived about 2,500 years ago.

**Capital**: The town or city where people who rule the country meet.

**Chopsticks**: Two long sticks that are used for eating food. Both chopsticks are held between the fingers of one hand.

**Crops**: Plants that farmers grow and sell.

**Embroidery**: Patterns that people sew into material with coloured thread.

**Festival**: A time when people remember something special that happened in the past, or a special time of the year.

**Gymnastics**: A sport which includes exercises on mats, bars and ropes, in a gym.

**Judo**: A sport which teaches you how to defend yourself without using weapons.

**Native**: Someone who was born in the country where they live.

**Pagoda**: A special building which looks like a tower. Pagodas are often beautifully decorated.

**P.S.**: This stands for Post Script. A postscript is the part of a letter or card which is added at the end, after the person has signed it.

**Republic**: A country where the people choose their leaders. A republic does not have a king or a queen.

**Temple**: A building where people go to pray.

**Traditional**: Something which has been done in the same way for a long time in the past.

**Tricycle**: A bicycle which has three wheels.

# Index